Through the Milky Way on a PB&J

James McDonald

HOUSE OF LORE

Through the Milky Way on a PB&J

www.HouseofLore.net

First House of Lore paperback edition, 2013

ISBN 13: 978-0-9886598-3-4
ISBN 10: 0988659832

Book Website
www.SamiAndThomas.com

It was the day of all days,
At the Cottage Cove School,
Because a field trip was planned,
That all the kids knew would rule.

They were off to the city,
To see the planetarium.
It was Thomas's class,
With his sis and his mum.

"Does she have to stay with me,
When my class is around?"
Thomas asked to his mother,
As Sami's smile turned down.

"Why Thomas C. Lamb,
You know she loves you.
Is it such a bad thing,
She wants to do all that you do?"

"No, I guess that it's not,"
Thomas said to his mom.
"Come on little Sami,
But don't sing a song."

"I promise I won't,"
Sami said to Thomas,
As they both hurried off,
To get on the bus.

When the bus had arrived,
They all poured into line,
So they would all get a chance,
At expanding their minds.

Across the space bridge they walked,
Then they all gathered round...
Whooosh! The room went dark.
And there wasn't a sound.

"Greetings today,
To all of you from Earth.
My name is Michelle,
And I come from Perth."

Then Michelle pushed some buttons,
And all the planets showed up,
And Sami and Thomas,
Were simply awestruck.

"This is it Sami,"
Thomas whispered to her.
"Soon we'll be in space."
And Sami's nod did concur.

So the fieldtrip went on,
And Thomas was taking good notes,
All the while Sami kept watch,
And hummed a few notes.

That night in his bedroom,
The two went over plans,
Of a two seated spacecraft,
That ran on Mom's jams.

"Is tomorrow the day?"
Sami asked as she played.
Then Thomas he nodded,
And said, "We'll be well on our way."

The next day was a best one,
Because it was the last day of school,
And Sami and Thomas,
Were on their bikes looking cool.

They had just been let out,
And were headed back home,
To make good on their plans,
That into space they would roam.

To the tree house they went,
As their mom came outside.
"Be careful up there,"
She smiled and sighed.

"I've got lunch for you both,"
She yelled up to them.
"Shall I assume that it's the same old,
PB&J again?"

"Yes please Mom," they said,
Smiling down from their fort.
Just what they were up to,
They would never report.

As their mom went inside,
They quickly ate up their lunch,
But Sami wasn't hungry,
So she saved half to munch.

"Are you ready to go?"
Thomas asked to Sami.
"You bet I am Thomas!"
"Then into space we will be."

So the brother and sister,
Climbed aboard their spaceship,
And they started the adventure,
Of their space-age day trip.

From the playhouse they shot,
Like an arrow in flight,
And up through the clouds,
So as to be out of sight.

"I think it's holding up good,"
Thomas smiled with pride.
To which Sami agreed,
And said, "It's a very smooth ride."

Then the light fell away,
As their ship entered space,
And the kids both felt different,
In this gravity free place.

"So where will it be,
Towards the sun and the heat?
Or the cold space of Pluto,
Where who knows what we'll meet?"

Sami thought for a second,
And said, "Pluto Please.
Because I hate getting hot,
And I'd much rather freeze."

"There'll be no freezing here,
Because I've packed us space suits,
That will save us from frost bite,
From our helmets to our boots."

"Well isn't that perfect,"
Sami said to Thomas.
"You're truly a genius,"
Which made Thomas blush.

"Well Sami you're smart,
And your singing's the best."
So the brother and sister,
Knew they were both very blessed.

"Could we go to the sun,
And then out to Pluto?"
Sami asked curiously,
And Thomas said, "Let's go."

So the ship set its course,
For our celestial star,
And they were there in a second,
Because it wasn't that far.

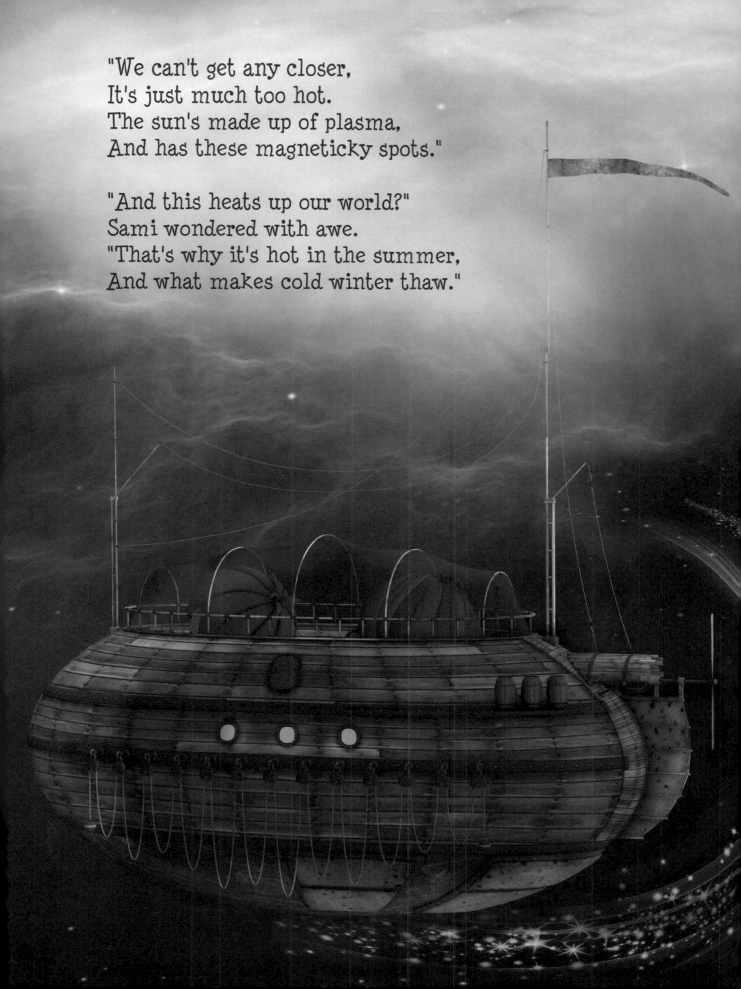

"We can't get any closer,
It's just much too hot.
The sun's made up of plasma,
And has these magneticky spots."

"And this heats up our world?"
Sami wondered with awe.
"That's why it's hot in the summer,
And what makes cold winter thaw."

Then they headed to Mercury,
The smallest planet around,
Whose surface is rocky,
And has a metallicky ground.

"The core's made up of iron,
And there are craters about,
But there's no air to breathe there,"
Sami said with a shout.

"And next up is Venus,"
Thomas said with delight.
"It's as bright as the moon,
On a cold winter's night."

Then they roared on to Earth,
With its beautiful blue,
"I sure love our planet Sami."
And Sami said, "Me too."

"The blue's from the water,
And the white is the clouds,"
Sami looked very proudly,
Speaking her knowledge out loud.

"Yes Sami that's true,
And there's a sphere around it,
That deflects lots of space gunk,
So that we barely get hit."

Then the ship passed by Mars,
And its two moons that go round.
"It looks red like that,
Because of the iron on the ground."

"It has mountains and valleys,
And there's even water about.
But I don't think the rivers,
Would hold any trout."

As the ship ventured on,
It was Jupiter next.
"They call it a gas giant."
Which made Sami perplexed.

"It's Hydrogen and Helium,
They're both a bit like air.
You can't visibly see them,
So you just know they're there."

And then the ringed planet came,
And Sami sang with much joy.
"It's Saturn my brother!
Like your plasticky toy."

"I do like this planet,"
Thomas said with a smile.
"It's nine times the Earth's size,
And the rings go on for miles."

"The planet Uranus,
Is as cold as they get.
And the pictures from satellites,
Show us just a blue blip."

"It takes 84 years,
For it to go around the sun."
And then Sami told Thomas,
"That doesn't sound like much fun."

The two journeyed on,
To the planet so blue.
"Neptune is the next one?"
Sami asked, "Isn't that true?"

Thomas smiled at Sami,
And said, "Yes indeed.
We've one left to go,
I say we've made some great speed."

And then Sami asked Thomas,
"Can we land on Pluto?"
And with a super big smile,
Thomas yelled out, "Let's GO!"

So they guided their ship,
To the barren waste land,
And they put on their space suits,
For an adventure so grand.

"You first my brother,
Because I'm scared without you."
So Thomas stepped out,
To a world totally new.

"We did it dear Sami!
It's just you and I.
Let's plant our flag here,
So all see it fly."

Then they got out their flag,
And they planted it down.
And that's when they heard it,
What sounded like someone around.

"Don't say a word,"
Thomas said to Sami.
"Let's head back to the ship,
Because there's more here than we."

Just then from behind,
An old broken grey rock,
Came a cute little creature,
Who waddled when he walked.

"Awww... Isn't he cute.
Can we take him back home?"
Sami asked Thomas,
As he let out a groan.

"Mom and Dad would be angry,
And tell us he just cannot stay.
Because Vesters and Petey,
Would have it no other way."

Then the creature approached,
And it held out its hand,
And showed them its ship,
Wrecked in the Plutoian sand.

"You see he is stranded,"
Sami said very sad.
"We can't leave him here,
Because that would be very bad."

"Fine," said Thomas,
As they boarded their ship.
"We'll try to find his home,
But it can't be a long trip."

"Thank you dear brother!
You're the kindest indeed."
Then the ship shot off Pluto,
At an incredible speed.

"So where do you live?"
Thomas said to the creature.
And that's when it smiled,
And pointed to a tiny space feature.

"Is that a planet out there?"
Sami asked to Thomas.
"Well, I guess we'll find out,
So we can stop all this fuss."

And so further away,
Than any human has gone,
The ship ventured forth,
Into a historic new dawn.

"What can we call you?"
Sami asked looking up.
Then it chirped and it smiled,
And she said, "I know! Space Pup."

Then the chirping and pointing,
Turned into sort of a scream,
As they came to a planet,
That was covered in steam.

"Space Pup must live there,"
Sami said pointing out.
"Then that's where we're headed,"
Thomas said with no doubt.

Through the steam and the smoke,
The ship entered a beautiful place,
Which was home to Space Pup,
And all of its race.

There were clouds all around,
And a sun made it bright.
With a jungly surface,
It all looked very right.

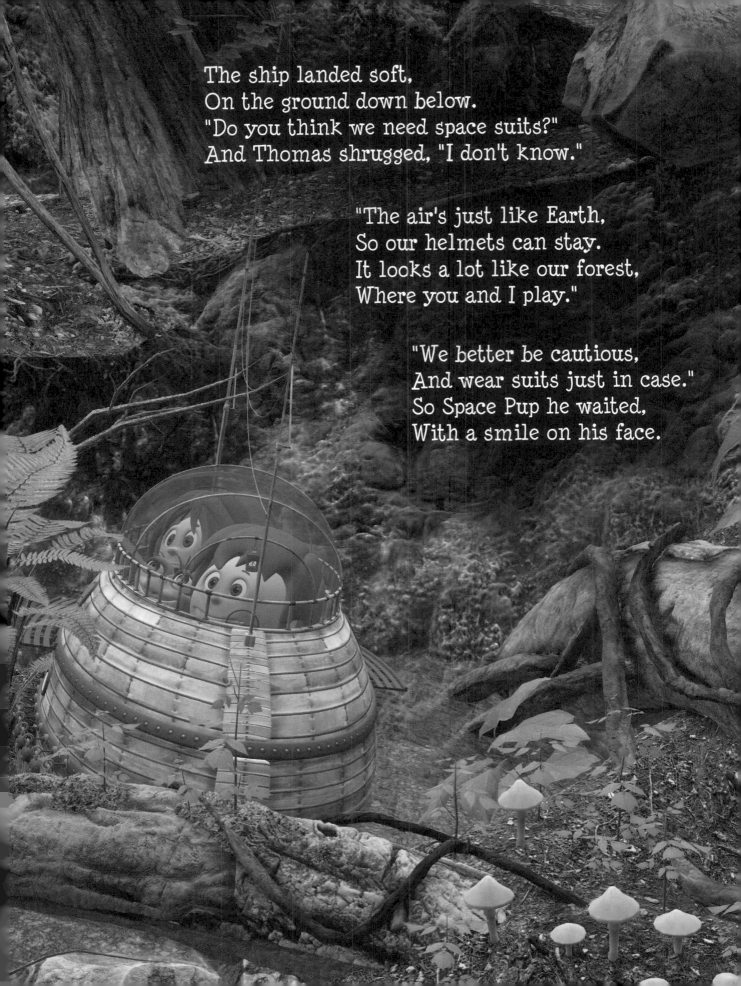

The ship landed soft,
On the ground down below.
"Do you think we need space suits?"
And Thomas shrugged, "I don't know."

"The air's just like Earth,
So our helmets can stay.
It looks a lot like our forest,
Where you and I play."

"We better be cautious,
And wear suits just in case."
So Space Pup he waited,
With a smile on his face.

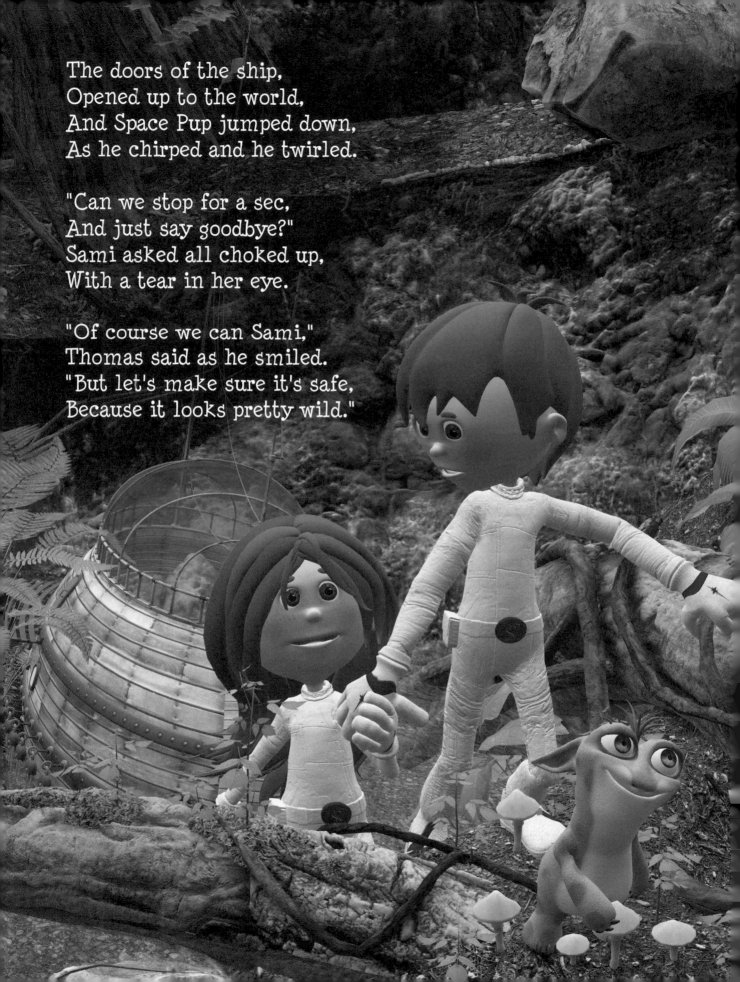

The doors of the ship,
Opened up to the world,
And Space Pup jumped down,
As he chirped and he twirled.

"Can we stop for a sec,
And just say goodbye?"
Sami asked all choked up,
With a tear in her eye.

"Of course we can Sami,"
Thomas said as he smiled.
"But let's make sure it's safe,
Because it looks pretty wild."

Just then there were noises,
Coming from all around,
And Sami and Thomas,
Made not one tiny sound.

"I'm scared dearest brother.
I think we'd better get gone."
And that's when they heard it,
A most beautiful song.

From the jungle emerged,
All Space Pup's family.
They were all so adorable,
Even the ones in a tree.

Then Space Pup approached,
And it held out its hand,
As if to thank Sami and Thomas,
For the return to its land.

"Well we better get going,
Because we cannot be late.
We've got to be home,
For our dinner-time plate."

So the brother and sister,
Stepped aboard their spaceship,
But when they tried to go home,
The ship had lost all its zip.

"I guess I didn't really plan,
That we'd travel this far.
Beyond planet Pluto,
To a new distant star."

"I'm sorry my sister,
But I think that we're stuck.
On this planet of space pups,
We've hit a bit of bad luck."

"Well at least they're all friendly,"
Sami said with a smile.
So the brother and sister,
Realized they'd be there a while.

"I'm already hungry,"
Sami said looking sad.
But just then she remembered,
What in her backpack she had.

So she pulled out her sandwich,
And started unwrapping it slow,
But then Thomas looked over,
And yelled to her "NOOO!"

"You've done it my sister!
You've found our way home!
Because that PB&J,
Will allow our spaceship to roam!"

Thomas grabbed up the sandwich,
And he fueled up the ship,
Then he pushed down some buttons,
And they were ready to rip.

With goodbyes all about,
And some shouts of Hurray,
The kids boarded their ship,
And were well on their way.

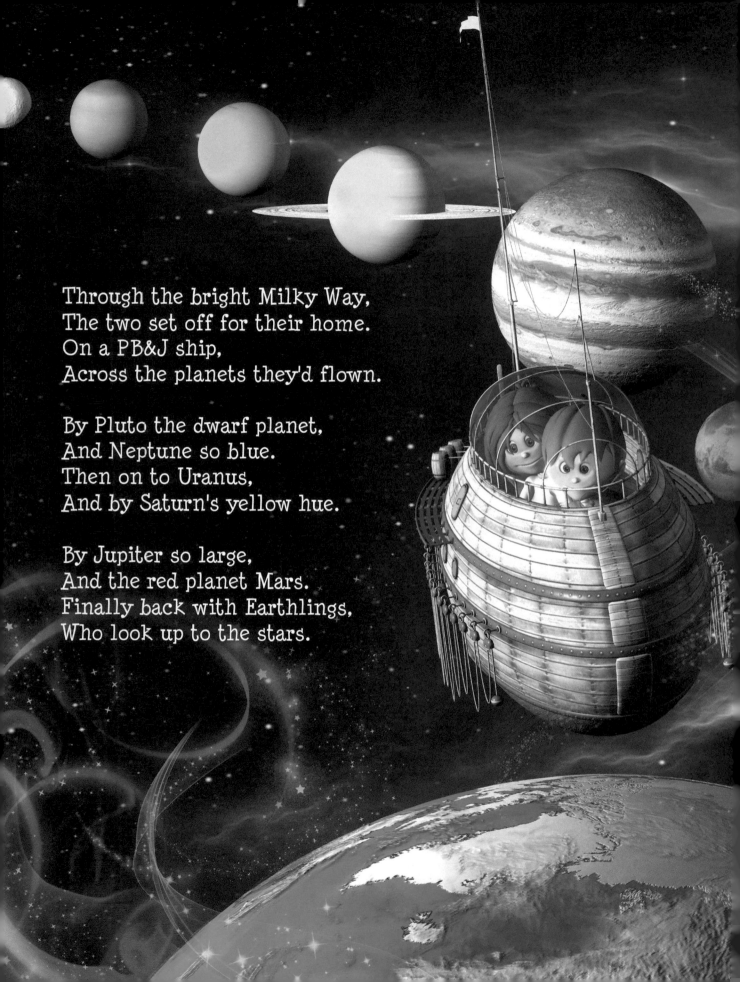

Through the bright Milky Way,
The two set off for their home.
On a PB&J ship,
Across the planets they'd flown.

By Pluto the dwarf planet,
And Neptune so blue.
Then on to Uranus,
And by Saturn's yellow hue.

By Jupiter so large,
And the red planet Mars.
Finally back with Earthlings,
Who look up to the stars.

They entered the atmosphere,
And the ship stood up strong,
Flying back to their tree house,
While Sami sang songs.

"We did it my brother!"
Sami shouted out loud.
Just then came their mom,
"Come on inside now."

And so the brother and sister,
Through the Milky Way flew,
On a PB&J ship,
That had seats just for two.

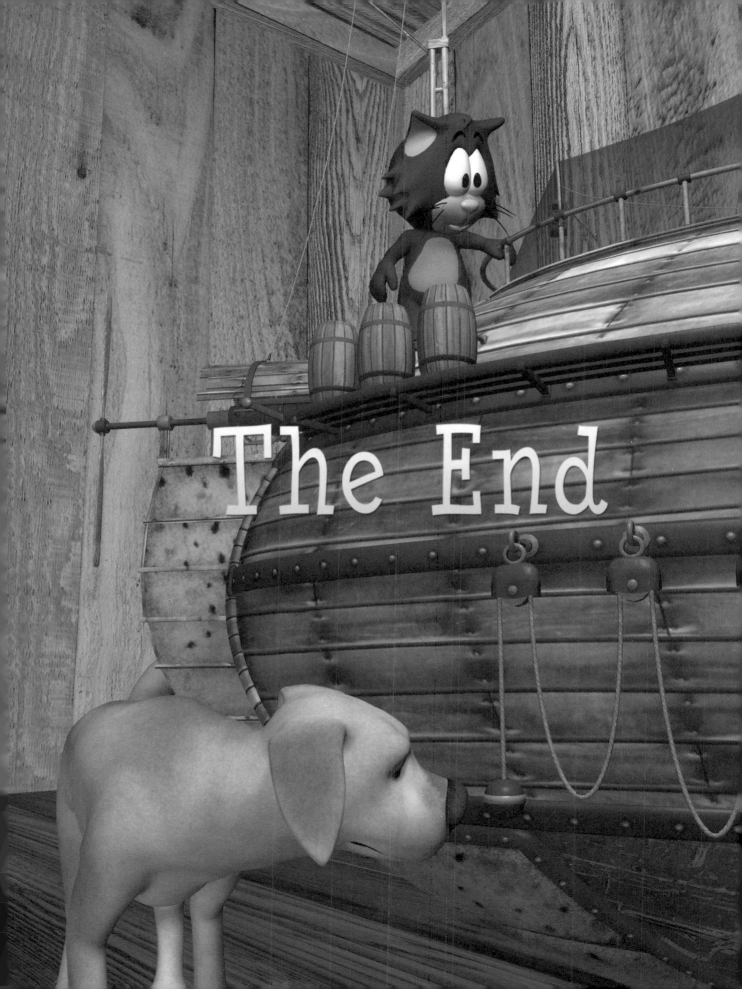

Made in the USA
San Bernardino, CA
22 December 2013